Instant Microsoft SQL Server Analysis Services 2012 Dimensions and Cube

Learn how to build dimensions and cubes in a SQL Server 2012 development environment

Anurag Acharya

BIRMINGHAM - MUMBAI

Instant Microsoft SQL Server Analysis Services 2012 Dimensions and Cube

First published: August 2013

Production Reference: 1230813

Published by Packt Publishing Ltd.
Livery Place
35 Livery Street
Birmingham B3 2PB, UK.

ISBN 978-1-84968-872-7

www.packtpub.com

Credits

Author
  Anurag Acharya

Reviewer
  Satishbabu Gunukula

Acquisition Editor
  Andrew Duckworth

Commissioning Editor
  Yogesh Dalvi

Technical Editors
  Amit Ramadas
  Jalasha D'costa

Project Coordinator
  Amigya Khurana

Proofreader
  Jonathan Todd

Production Coordinator
  Pooja Chiplunkar

Cover Work
  Pooja Chiplunkar

Cover Image
  Conidon Miranda

About the Author

Anurag Acharya is an information security researcher, a consultant, and an expert in networks and server security. He has eight years' practical experience with different vendor technologies, such as Cisco, HP, IBM, Avaya, Red Hat, Microsoft Servers, and network security software such as Panda Firewall. He has a keen interest in working with different technologies. He started his career as a hardware and network engineer, and later he worked as a corporate trainer. He trained hundreds of students, engineers, and government employees in Microsoft Servers (Exchange, Threat Management, Voice, and SQL). As his latest Network profile, he managed some datacenter production servers at a reputed company. He also has experience with Active Directory, DHCP, DNS servers, web servers, application servers, Exchange Servers, SharePoint Servers, database servers, and so on with their administration, monitoring, and security. He has a few international credentials including MCSE, MCSA Security, MCSA Exchange, MCITP Enterprise, MCSA on Core Server, CCNA, CCNA Security, CCNP, CCNP Security, CEH, and ACSE (IT security and ethical hacking). Currently, he is working as a freelance ethical hacking trainer and penetration tester with several institutes. He also provides private training online as well as offline. Soon, he will launch a website, www.mrintruder.com, through which he hopes to help students and professionals to explore their knowledge in different technologies.

He is also in the process of writing two books on Microsoft technologies: Windows Server 2012 and Exchange Server 2013. These books help the server administrators to manage, administrate, and upgrade servers on Windows Server 2012 and Exchange Server 2013.

I would like to thank my mother who has always been supportive and has let me do whatever I want. She has 20 years' experience in writing books and translating them, along with proofreading. She has also written many books. Special thanks to my best friend Jass. She has always motivated me to lead life with self-confidence, self-respect, and self-power. I would also like to thank my gurus Sachin and Harvinder Dhot. Sachin trained me in Microsoft Server technologies and Harvinder Dhot trained me in Cisco. Both of them have always motivated me to work hard to achieve success. Finally, I would like to thank everyone who encouraged me.

About the Reviewer

Satishbabu Gunukula has more than 13 years of experience in the IT industry. He has extensive experience in SQL Server and Oracle Database technologies, and is specialized in high-availability solutions, such as SQL Server Cluster, Oracle RAC, Data Guard, and Grid Control. He has experience on a wide range of products, such as Essbase, Hyperion, Agile, SAP Basis, MySQL, Linux, Windows, SSAS, SSRS, and Business Apps admin, and he has implemented many business-critical systems for Fortune 500 and 1000 companies.

Satishbabu Gunukula has a Master's degree in Computer Application. He has published several articles for technical journals, blogs, and has reviewed several books for Packt Publishing. He has been honored with the prestigious Oracle ACE award. He shares his knowledge on his websites at http://sqlserver-expert.com and http://www.oracleracexpert.com.

www.packtpub.com

Support files, eBooks, discount offers and more

You might want to visit www.packtpub.com for support files and downloads related to your book.

Did you know that Packt offers eBook versions of every book published, with PDF and ePub files available? You can upgrade to the eBook version at www.packtpub.com and as a print book customer, you are entitled to a discount on the eBook copy. Get in touch with us at service@packtpub.com for more details.

At www.packtpub.com, you can also read a collection of free technical articles, sign up for a range of free newsletters and receive exclusive discounts and offers on Packt books and eBooks.

packtlib.packtpub.com

Do you need instant solutions to your IT questions? PacktLib is Packt's online digital book library. Here, you can access, read, and search across Packt's entire library of books.

Why Subscribe?

- ✦ Fully searchable across every book published by Packt
- ✦ Copy and paste, print and bookmark content
- ✦ On demand and accessible via web browser

Free Access for Packt account holders

If you have an account with Packt at www.packtpub.com, you can use this to access PacktLib today and view nine entirely free books. Simply use your login credentials for immediate access.

Table of Contents

Instant Microsoft SQL Server Analysis Services 2012 Dimensions and Cube

Welcome to *Instant Microsoft SQL Server Analysis Services 2012 Dimensions and Cube*. This book has been especially created to provide you with all the information that you need to get set up with SQL Server 2012. You will learn the basics of SQL Server 2012, get started with installation, administrations, and some essential knowledge of SQL Server 2012 features and services with dimensions and cube development.

This document contains the following sections:

So, what are SSAS 2012 dimensions and cube? talks about the special new features and services present, what you can do with them, and why they're so great.

Installation helps you learn how to download and install the SQL Server 2012 with graphical and core installation, and then set it up so that you can use it as soon as possible.

Quick start - getting started with the peripherals of SSAS 2012 helps you get started with peripherals of SSAS 2012 and also covers some of the kick-start topics that are essential to start the journey with SQL Server 2012.

Top 5 features you need to know about helps you learn how to perform certain tasks using the most important features of SQL Server 2012. By the end of this section, you will be able to perform the following tasks: core installation of SQL Server 2012, security consideration during the installment, installing additional features and services, creating the dimension in SQL Server developing environment, and creating the cube in development with the Cube Wizard.

People and places you should get to know lets you know that every open source project that is centered around a community. This section also provides you with many useful links to the project page and forums.

So, what are SSAS 2012 dimensions and cube?

In this section we will learn what SSAS 2012 is, why we need it, and then thread on a bit of description of the SSAS history. We will also discuss the architecture of SSAS 2012 with their data models, the future of SSAS 2012, along with what's new in SSAS 2012. After that we will talk about the SSAS dimensions and cube.

What is SSAS?

SQL Server Analysis Services is an online analytical processing tool that highly boosts the different types of SQL queries and calculations that are accepted in the business intelligence environment. It looks like a relation database, but it has differences. SSAS does not replace the requirement of relational databases, but if you combine the two, it would help to develop the business intelligence solutions.

Why do we need SSAS?

SSAS provide a very clear graphical interface for the end users to build queries. It is a kind of cache that we can use to speed up reporting. In most real scenarios where SSAS is used, there is a full copy of the data in the data warehouse. All reporting and analytic queries are run against SSAS rather than against the relational database. Today's modern relational databases include many features specifically aimed at BI reporting. SSAS are database services specifically designed for this type of workload, and in most cases it has achieved much better query performance.

SSAS 2012 architecture

In this section we will explain about the architecture of SSAS. The first and most important point to make about SSAS 2012 is that it is really two products in one package. It has had a few advancements relating to performance, scalability, and manageability. This new version of SSAS that closely resembles PowerPivot uses the **tabular model**. When installing SSAS, we must select either the tabular model or multidimensional model for installing an instance that runs inside the server; both data models are developed under the same code but sometimes both are treated separately. The concepts included in designing both data models are different, and we can't turn a tabular database into a multidimensional database, or vice versa without rebuilding everything from the start. The main point of view of the end users is that both data models do almost the same things and appear almost equally when used through a client tool such as Excel.

The tabular model

A concept of building a database using the tabular model is very similar to building it in a relational database. An instance of Analysis Services can hold many databases, and each database can be looked upon as a self-contained collection of objects and data relating to a single business solution. If we are writing reports or analyzing data and we find that we need to run queries on multiple databases, we probably have made a design mistake somewhere because everything we need should be contained within an individual database. Tabular models are designed by using **SQL Server Data Tools** (**SSDT**), and a data project in SSDT mapping onto a database in Analysis Services.

The multidimensional model

This data model is very similar to the tabular model. Data is managed in databases, and databases are designed in SSDT, which are in turn managed by using SQL Server Management Studio. The differences may become similar below the database level, where the multidimensional data model rather than relational concepts are accepted. In the multidimensional model, data is modeled as a series of cubes and dimensions and not tables.

The future of Analysis Services

We have two data models inside SSAS, along with two query and calculation languages; it is clearly not an ideal state of affairs. It means we have to select a data model to use at the start of our project, when we might not even know enough about our need to gauge which one is appropriate. It also means that anyone who decides to specialize in SSAS has to learn two technologies. Microsoft has very clearly said that the multidimensional model is not scrapped and that the tabular model is not its replacement. It is just like saying that the new advanced features for the multidimensional data model will be released in future versions of SSAS. The fact that the tabular and multidimensional data models share some of the same code suggests that some new features could easily be developed for both models simultaneously.

What's new in SSAS 2012?

As we know, there is no easy way of transferring a multidimensional data model into a tabular data model. We may have many tools in the market that claim to make this transition with a few mouse clicks, but such tools could only ever work for very simple multidimensional data models and would not save much development time. Therefore, if we already have a mature multidimensional implementation and the in-house skills to develop and maintain it, we may find the following improvements in SSAS 2012 useful.

Ease of use

If we are starting an SSAS 2012 project with no previous multidimensional or OLAP experience, it is very likely that we will find a tabular model much easier to learn than a multidimensional one. Not only are the concepts much easier to understand, especially if we are used to working with relational databases, but also the development process is much more straightforward and there are far fewer features to learn.

Compatibility with PowerPivot

The tabular data model and PowerPivot are the same in the way their models are designed. The user interfaces used are practically the same, as both the interfaces use DAX. PowerPivot models can be imported into SQL Server Data Tools to generate a tabular model, although the process does not work the other way around, and a tabular model cannot be converted to a PowerPivot model.

Processing performance characteristics

If we compare the processing performance of the multidimensional and tabular data models, that will become difficult. It may be slower to process a large table following the tabular data model than the equivalent measure group in a multidimensional one because a tabular data model can't process partitions in the same table at the same time, whereas a multidimensional model can process partitions in the same measure group at the same time.

What is SSAS dimension?

A database dimension is a collection of related objects; in other words, attributes; they provide the information about fact data in one or more cubes. Typical attributes in a product dimension are product name, product category, line, size, and price. Attributes can be organized into user-defined hierarchies that provide the paths to assist users when they browse through the data in a cube. By default these attributes are visible as attribute hierarchies, and they can be used to understand fact data in a cube.

What is SSAS cube?

A cube is a multidimensional structure that contains information for analytical purposes; the main constituents of a cube are **dimensions** and **measures**. Dimensions define the structure of a cube that you use to slice and dice over, and measures provide the aggregated numerical values of interest to the end user. As a logical structure, a cube allows a client application to retrieve values—of measures—as if they are contained in cells in the cube. The cells are defined for every possible summarized value. A cell, in the cube, is defined by the intersection of dimension members and contains the aggregated values of the measures at that specific intersection.

Installation

In this section we will learn how to design the SQL Server installation. Before installing SQL Server and when deploying the server, we will check the security considerations.

Step 1 – designing the installation

When we deploy SQL Server in our organization, we will firstly always design those features and components that are required, and install those that fulfill the organization demand. In SQL Server 2012, we have two types of features: **shared features** and **instance features.**

Step 2 – deploying SQL Server 2012

Here, we will learn about the hardware and software requirements for the SQL Server 2012 deployment along with a link where we can download SQL Server.

What do we need?

The hardware requirements are as follows:

✦   Intel XEON, AMD athlon64, AMD Opteron, Intel Pentium IV 64-bit supported is required

✦   Minimum 1.0 GHz, recommended processor 2.0 GHz or faster

✦   Minimum 1 GB RAM, recommended is 4 GB or more

The software requirements are as follows:

✦   Windows Server 2008 R2 SP1 Datacenter, Enterprise, Standard, and Web 64-bit editions.

✦   Install .NET 3.5 SP1 or .NET 4.0. It gets automatically downloaded and deployed with SQL Server 2012 setup files, and on Window Power Shell 2.0 or Internet Explorer.

We can download the SQL Server 2012 SP1 Enterprise edition from the official Microsoft website at http://www.microsoft.com/betaexperience/pd/SQL2012EvalCTA/enus/default.aspx.

When we click on the link given, we are redirected to the download page. There we can see both the 32-bit and 64-bit versions. Just select the version with the language and download it.

Deployment of SQL Server 2012

The following steps will guide you through the deployment of SQL Server 2012:

1. First, open the DVD of SQL Server and go to the folder where all the installation files are placed. After that, right-click on the `setup` file and start the installation. One thing we should remember is that the administrator should have administrative privileges, and then execute the EXE file by clicking on **Run As Administrator**, as shown in the following screenshot:

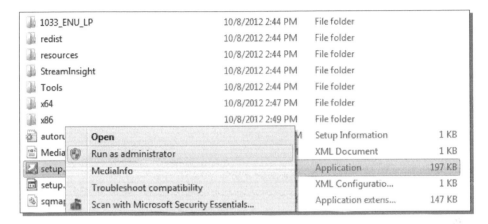

2. Once our prerequisites have been successfully set up, a server restart is required. If our prerequisites are already installed, continue with the installation process.

3. Next, you should choose the processor type: 32 bit or 64 bit. By default, 32 bit is selected, but then again you can choose the processor type depending on the scenario or your organizational needs.

4. From the **SQL Server Installation Center** wizard, we choose the first option, **New SQL Server stand-alone installation or add features to an existing Installation**:

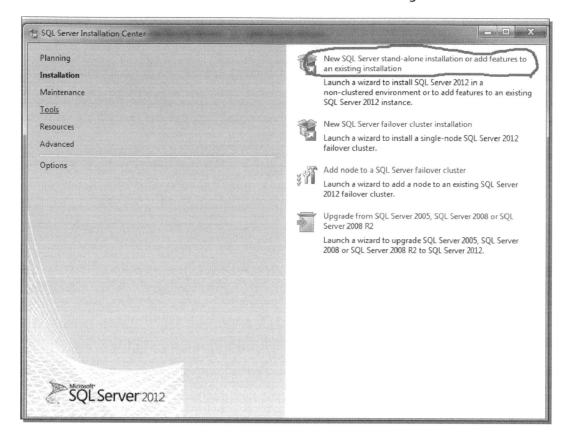

5. After this we will see the **Setup Support Rules** page that diagnoses the problems that may occur when we deploy the SQL Server setup files. We must correct the failure if there are any before the setup continues; if there is no issue, we can continue with the installation. Take a look at the following screenshot:

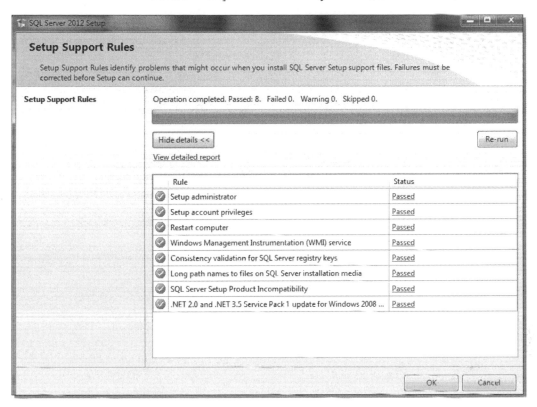

6. In the **Product Key** section, enter the product key of SQL Server 2012. We can choose **Installation Evaluation Edition**, or if we want a specific version, we must enter the product key number. Choose Installation Evaluation Edition, and then click on **Next** to continue the deployment.

> If you are installing the Evaluation Edition, you can upgrade to any other version by using the edition upgrade wizard. Once upgraded from Evaluation to Enterprise, or so on, to another available version, you can't downgrade. In such a case, you should uninstall SQL Server and reinstall it.

7. In the **License Terms** section, go through the entire licensing terms, and then check the two checkboxes at the bottom of the screen to accept the licensing terms and conditions and send the used data to Microsoft's feature usage data and include information of the hardware configuration and how you use SQL Server and its component. Finally, click on **Next**.

8. After installing the setup files, we will again see the **Setup Support Rules** screen and again check the issues mentioned. If you get an error regarding the firewall, disable the firewall during the installation and enable it after the complete installation has taken place. Lastly, click on **Next**.

9. In the **Setup Role** wizard, select the option **SQL Server Feature Installation** to separately select the feature components to be installed, or select a particular role to deploy a specific configuration. We can see the three options, but we select the first option and then click on **Next**, as shown in the following screenshot:

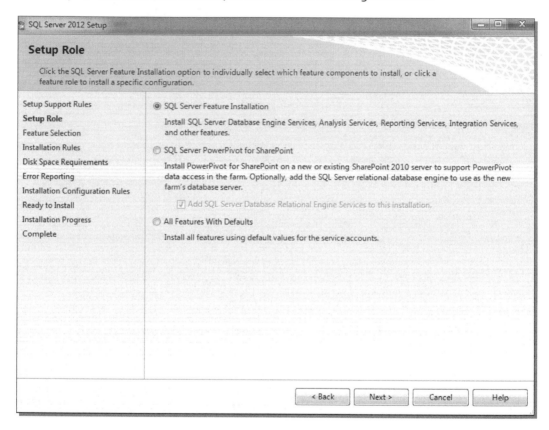

10. Now we see the **Feature Selection** wizard, where all the services available in SQL Server 2012 are displayed. The following screenshot shows the different segments available within SQL Server:

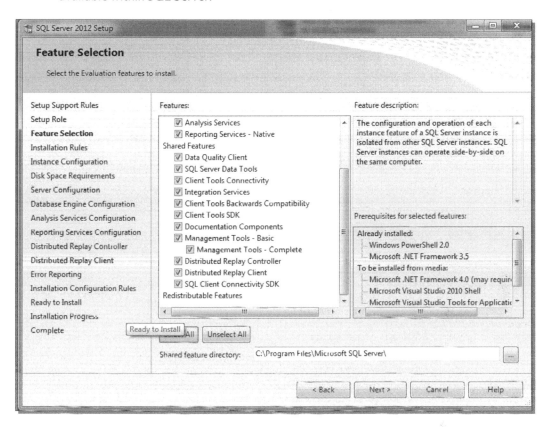

11. In the **Installation Rules** section, we see the setup running rules that helps us decide if deployment will be blocked. Click on **Next** to continue.

12. On the **Instance Configuration** screen, we put the instance name and ID for the SQL Server new instance and click on **Next**:

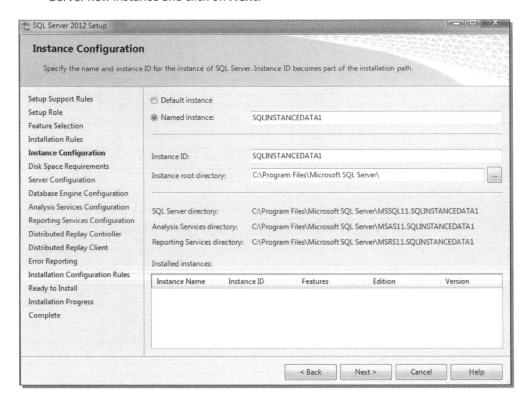

13. In the **Disk Space Requirements** section, we will be able to check the amount of data space that is needed for the deployment. Click on **Next**.

14. On the **Server Configuration** page, we see two tabs: **Service Account** and **Collation Configuration**. In the **Service Account** tab, we can configure the service accounts that run under the SQL instance service. It should be running, and should also specify the startup type for specific SQL Server services. In the **Collations Configuration** tab, we can configure the collation for database engine services and Analysis Services, or we can leave the default value as per the OS. Click on **Next**.

15. On the **Database Engine Configuration** page, we can configure the authentication mode and specify the administrator to the database engine, data directories, and file stream through the **Account Provisioning** option. For practice, the best to use is the mixed mode. Configure the passwords for the database administrator.

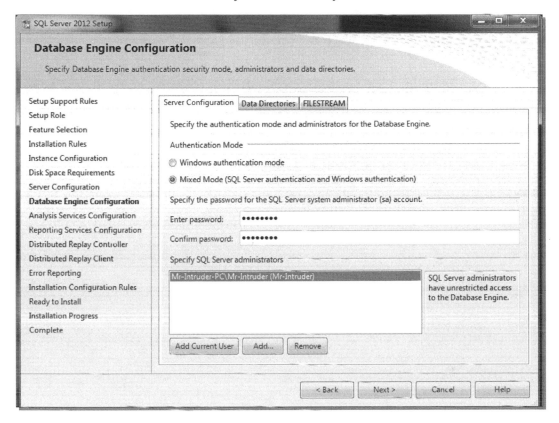

On the preceding screen we have three tabs. Under **Data Directories**, we can configure the path of where the database data and logfiles should be stored so that it will improve server performance.

16. In the **FILESTREAM** tab, we can configure the file stream of SQL Server. There are three types of file stream configurations:

   ° **Enable FILESTREAM for Transact-SQL access**

   ° **Enable FILESTREAM for file I/O streaming access**

   ° **Allow remote clients to have streaming access to FILESTREAM data**

17. On the **Analysis Services Configuration** page, we can configure the Analysis Services administrator and data directories. We can also add the administrators who have permission on Analysis Services through the **Account Provisioning** option. We can define data recovery, the logfile directory, and the temp and backup directories for Analysis Services in the **Data Directories** tab. Click on **Next**:

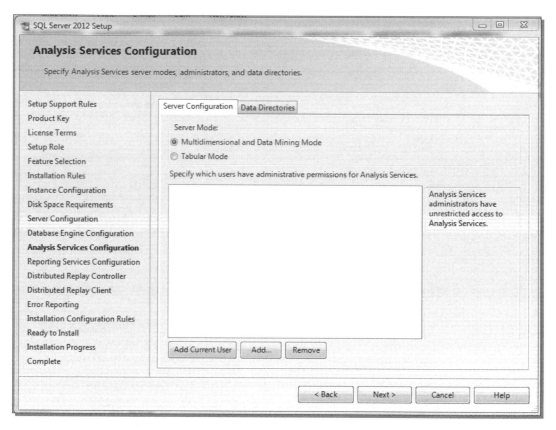

18. On the **Reporting Services Configuration** page, we see two types of different choices, which are applicable when configuring the Reporting Services. They are as follows:

    ○ **Reporting Service Native Mode**: Under this mode we have two suboptions:

        ○ **Install and configure**

        ○ **Install only**

    ○ **Reporting Services SharePoint Integrated Mode**: In this mode we have only one option:

        ○ **Install only**

19. Choose the suitable Reporting Service configuration option and click on **Next**, as shown in the following screenshot:

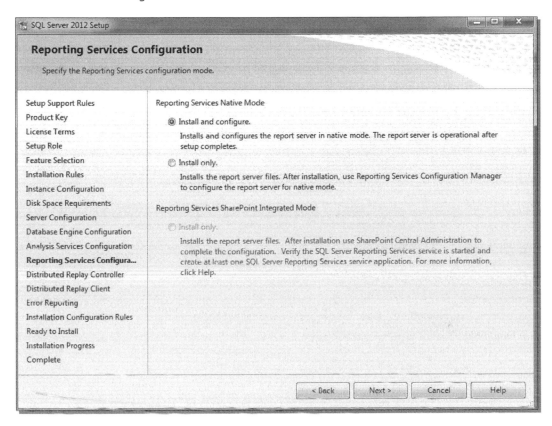

20. In **Distributed Replay Controller**, we can decide on the users and assign administrative permissions to them for the Distributed Replay Client Service. They automatically have unlimited access to Distributed Replay Client Service. Click on **Next**.

21. The **Distributed Replay Client** section specifies the controller name, the live directory, and the result directory location. The controller name is an optional parameter that we can leave blank. This client controller will then be connected to Distributed Replay Client Service. Click on **Next**.

22. In the **Error Reporting** section, select the checkbox to automatically send logs to Microsoft to improve the future release of the SQL Server service pack. Click on **Next**.

23. In the **Installation Configuration Rules** section, the setup will run rules to resolve any type of error, if the installation process will be blocked. In case there are any issues, they need to be fixed before continuing the deployment. Click on **Next**.

24. On the **Ready to Install** screen, we can quickly review the features that have been selected so far for the installation, and then click on the **Install** button to continue the deployment of SQL Server.

25. On the **Installation Progress** screen, we can monitor the progress of the SQL Server deployment. Click on **Next** to see the summary.

26. On the **Complete** screen, we can review the summary logs and location to click on the link that is given below on the screen. Once SQL Server is successfully installed, just click on the **Close** button to exit the SQL Server setup and click on **OK**.

Step 3 – confirming the security considerations before a SQL Server deployment

Security is an essential part of every business, organization, or product. Through smooth deployment and use of the best practices, we can escape much of the security vulnerabilities. Here we discuss security practices that we should consider before the deployment of SQL Server.

Firewalls

Implementing firewalls is the best practice that provides security to the SQL Server deployment along with protection of data from hackers or intruders, but just implementation is not enough to protect data. We should follow some guidelines that make firewall security effective. They are as follows:

+ The firewall should be placed between the server and Internet.

+ Always enable the firewall; if in any case the firewall is turned off, immediately turn it on.

+ Create a separate zone in the network through the firewall and block all traffic. Only selective data should be allowed to enter in or exit out to/from the server or network.

+ When deploying SQL Server in the server-client environment, we should configure the internal firewall to allow Windows authentication.

+ In a multitier scenario, use a variety of firewalls to create screened subnets.

+ If our application uses distributed transactions, we should configure the firewall to allow MS DTC traffic to flow between the MS DTC instances.

Enlarging physical security

Physical security is also an essential part of any organization, which includes protection of personnel, hardware, programs, networks, and data from physical circumstances or events that could cause serious losses or damages in an organization. To improve the physical security of the SQL Server deployment, we should follow these norms:

+ Place the database servers in a room where only authorized persons can enter
+ The server room should be locked and should follow a flood detection and fire disclosure or suppressing system
+ Install the database in the secure zone of the corporate Internet, and make sure SQL Server is never directly connected to the Internet
+ Take a backup of the entire data server regularly (every day, if possible) and store the backup at a secure site location
+ Disable the portable drives and external drives, such as pen drives, external floppy drives, or any other type of portable devices

Running individual services

If we install and run separate SQL services, the risk of data theft is reduced. If any single service is compromised by intruders, the rest of the services could be compromised. The best practice is that we install and run the separate services with different authentication and parameters.

Disabling the NetBIOS and SMB

Unnecessary protocols, services, and ports, including NetBIOS and the **Server Message Block** (**SMB**) protocol, should be disabled on the network on which the database servers are placed.

NetBIOS use the following ports:

+ UDP 137 to NETBIOS name service
+ UDP 138 to NETBIOS datagram service
+ TCP 139 to NETBIOS session service

The SMB protocol uses the TCP 139 and 445 ports. IIS servers and Domain Name Servers don't require NetBIOS and SMB. On these servers both services and their ports should be disabled, as the user enumeration attack will be reduced.

Using NTFS for a secure filesystem

Choose the correct and secure filesystem for the SQL Server deployment. NTFS is the best filesystem for a SQL Server deployment because it is more stable and recoverable as compared to the FAT filesystem. NTFS provides the security and encryption, access control list on both levels; files and folders. We can implement the raid for demanding datafiles.

Step 4 – checking security considerations during or after deployment of SQL Server

During, or when we have completed, the deployment of SQL Server, we should check and implement the security consideration-related accounts and privilege modes, such as the ones given as follows:

+ **Service Accounts**: SQL Services run with the lowest possible privilege of local user accounts or domain user accounts.

+ **Privilege Mode**: For Windows and Kerberos privilege in order to connect to SQL Server.

+ **Secure Passwords**: Always assign a secure password to the SA account and an SQL Server login. We should enable the password policy to confirm the password length and expiration.

Quick start – getting started with the peripherals of SSAS 2012

In this section we will learn some additional peripherals of SQL Server 2012, which are used by analytical and reporting services in the SQL Server development environment. We will learn how to deploy and configure these components, why we need to install them, how to create the first SQL instance in the SQL development environment, and its administration and configuration. We will also learn about the administration of user management and server roles, and an overview of types of privileges that SQL Server supports. We will also delve into database users, contained users, and server-level roles (for example, fixed server roles, user-defined roles, database roles, and application roles). Lastly, we will look into developing and creating the dimensions and cubes in the SQL database server environment.

SQL Server 2012 supplementary peripherals

Here we will learn about reporting and analytical services, both the peripheral of SQL Server. We will learn how we can deploy and configure the additional components and their functions. We will also come to know about the multidimensional and tabular model along with the working of information services.

Analysis Services

This is an OLAP and highly optimized database tool for SQL queries and calculations that are common in the business intelligence environment. This can perform many tasks like a relational database, but a few aspects make this different from a relational database. Through the analytical services, we can easily develop the task of BI solving and not only reduce the IT department workload but also increase end user satisfaction as the user can now easily build the reports they want, and explore data at their own pace.

Deploying and configuring Analysis Services

When we deploy and configure Analysis Services, we follow the same steps as that of the deployment of SQL Server, which we have already discussed during the installation. We just make a few changes in the configuration during the deployment of Analysis Services.

 Whenever we deploy any additional features, service, or components after the completed SQL Server 2012 deployment, we always give the path of the setup files' folder after we click on **New SQL Server stand-alone installation and add new feature to an existing installation**.

Firstly, we must make some changes in the configuration in the **Installation Type** wizard, where we have two options. If we want to deploy Analysis Services with a new SQL instance, we select **Perform a new installation of SQL Server 2012**, or if we want to deploy Analysis Services on an existing instance, we select the **Add features to an existing instance of SQL Server 2012** option. The following screenshot shows the selection of the first option to deploy Analysis Services:

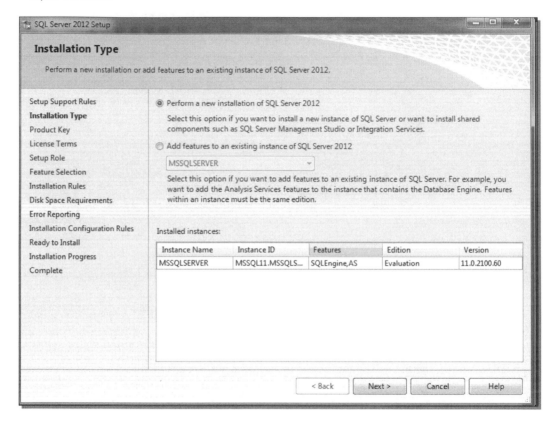

Second, we must select **Analysis Services** in the **Feature Selection** wizard, depending on the requirement. We can deploy Analysis Services individually or with other services; here we are installing individually:

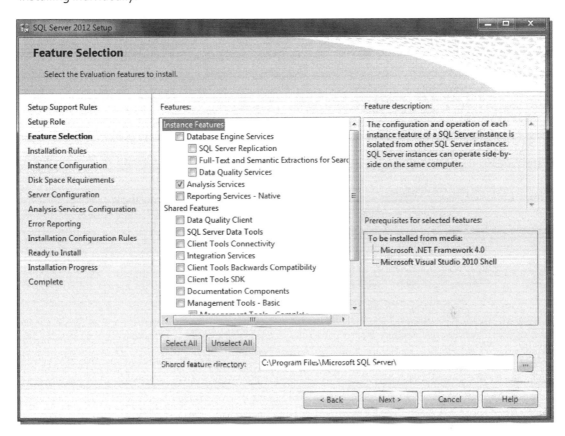

After this we must select the one mode that will work with each database instance of Analysis Services. The following screenshot shows the selection of **Multidimensional and Data Mining Mode**:

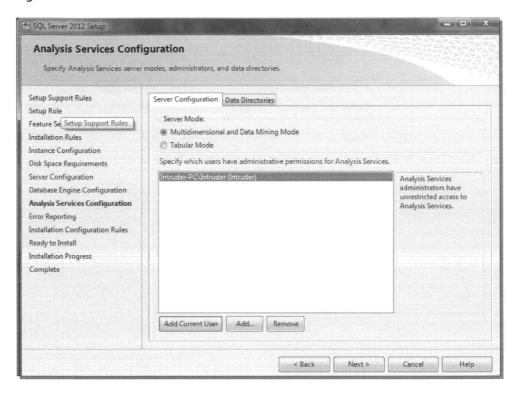

A particular mode should be selected for each instance. Note that we can use more than one mode for an instance, and for that we need to install the multiple Analysis Services database instance. SQL Server 2012 has two database models, and both the models have different features, which are given in detail in the following sections.

The tabular model

The tabular model comes inbuilt with SQL Server 2012. It works purely on a memory-based engine, which means it stores data on the disk. This comes in handy when we need to restart the service, or when it gets automatically restarted, so that the data is not lost. This model uses the compression algorithm and multiuser thread query processing. The xVelocity engine provides access to the tabular objects and data in a quick and efficient manner through client applications such as Power View and Microsoft Excel. The tabular model has been designed by **SQL Server Data Tools (SSDT)**, and it helps in designing a project in SSDT maps. Then after finishing the design, we must deploy that project on a database instance of Analysis Services. After deploying the project, we can execute the various commands to create a new database instance or alter the existing database instance in Analysis Services, with the data in tables organized according to the tabular model.

The multidimensional and data mining model

This model is a traditional Online Analytical Process cube model that has been used for more than 10 years now. This model stores data in cubes and dimensions and not in tables. Each cube creates more than one measure group, and those groups in a cube both map onto a single fact table. The multidimensional model is the direct successor of the previous version (the tabular model) of Analysis Services. This model enables fast performance of ad hoc queries on the business data, as it supports the native language MDX, which is traditionally used for defining queries and performing calculations. The MDX languages successfully support a large number of third-party software for Analysis Services.

Reporting Services

This is a server-client-based reporting platform that provides a very attractive, clear, and comprehensive functionality to view data. It also provides a functional set of tools for us to create, manage, and deliver reports, and an API that can be enabled by the developer in order to integrate and explore the data using a business mode application.

Deploying and building Reporting Services

When we deploy the inherent Reporting Services, we follow the same steps as that of the SQL Server 2012 deployment, which we already discussed in the *Installation* section. Here we will have to make some changes in the configuration based on these steps.

Firstly, we must make a few changes in the configuration in the **Installation Type** wizard, where we have two options. If we want to deploy Reporting Services with a native SQL instance, we need to select **Perform a new installation of SQL Server 2012**, or if we want to deploy Reporting Services on an existing instance, we need to select the **Add features to an existing instance of SQL Server 2012** option, as shown in the following screenshot:

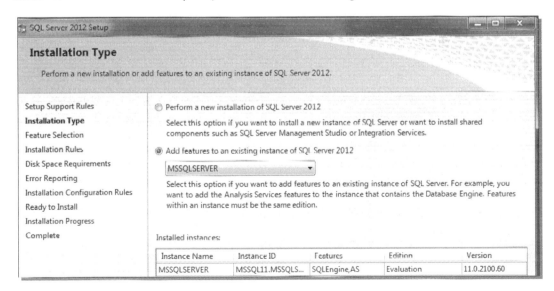

Next, we make changes in the **Feature Selection** wizard; we select **Reporting Services – Native** and continue the installation:

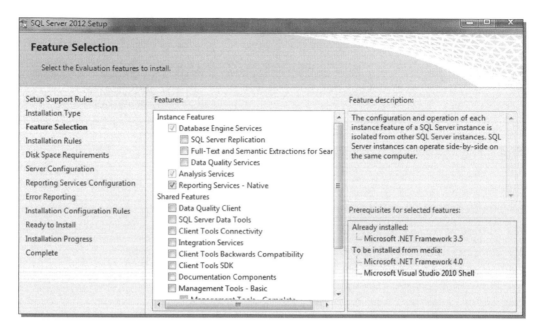

We also need to make changes in the **Reporting Services Configuration** wizard. We see that there are three options, with only one option highlighted and the remaining options grayed. This is because we are deploying Reporting Services on an existing SQL instance. The following screenshot shows the selection of the second option; click on **Next** to continue the deployment:

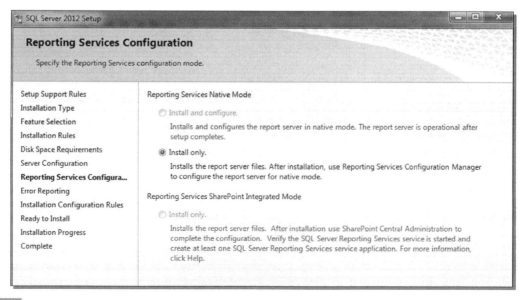

After completing the installation, we need to connect to Reporting Services through the configuration manager.

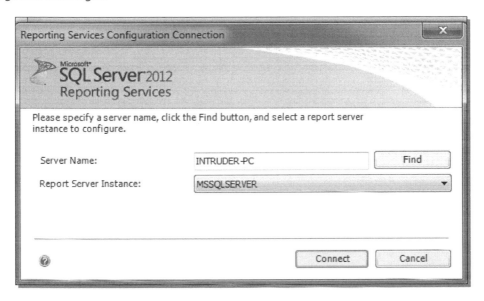

With regard to SQL Server Reporting Services, through **Reporting Services Configuration Manager**, and all the different configuration options, we can efficiently arrange Reporting Services.

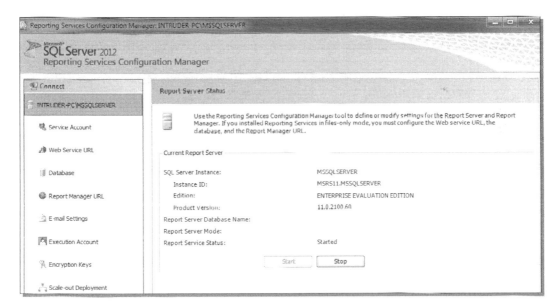

The following settings can be taken care of through the Reporting Services Configuration Manager:

+ The Reporting Services account
+ The TCP port, the URL web service, the IP address, the virtual directory, and SSL certificates
+ The database reporting server and database credential
+ The report manager URL
+ E-mail settings, which include the sender address, the current SMTP delivery method, and the SMTP server
+ Execution accounts
+ Backup and restore configurations along with update Reporting Services encryption keys
+ Scaling the installation

Administrating and creating a SQL Server instance

A SQL Server database instance is a complete SQL Server. We can deploy multiple instances on a hosted machine, but by default only one instance is created during installation. The rest of the installed instances are additional instances and are called **names instances**. SQL Server supports up to 50 instances of database engine services and up to 25 database instances of a failover cluster. We can deploy a separate utility of SQL Server with separate program files and directories, along with the SQL services individually or together on a specific instance. An administrator can assign the administrative rights on each SQL Server database instance.

We will now create and install the newly added SQL Server database engine instance with the name TESTINSTANCE1 in SQL Server 2012, by using the following steps:

1. Open the **SQL Server Installation Center** wizard from the **Configuration Tools** option of Microsoft SQL Server in the start menu, and then click on **Yes** when presented with the User Account dialog box.

2. Select the first option **New SQL Server stand-alone or add features to an existing installation**, and then click on **Next**.

3. Next, we will see the **Setup Support Rules** screen, which will identify the problems that might occur when we install the additional SQL Server instance. We must correct the errors occurring before completing the SQL Server database instance. If there are no issues, we can continue with the installation.

4. The installation then checks the updates; click on **Next** to proceed. Then, again, **Setup Support Rules** verifies all the steps, and you will have to click on **Next** to continue.

5. In the **Installation Type** wizard, choose the **Perform a new installation of SQL Server 2012** option and then click on **Next**.

6. In the **Product Key** section, we can enter the product key of SQL Server 2012. We can choose the Evaluation Edition, or if needed we can specify a particular version and enter its product key. Click on **Next** to continue the deployment.

7. In the **License Terms** section, accept the licensing terms and conditions and then click on **Next**.

8. In the **Setup Role** wizard, select the first option to separately select the feature component or role in order to install a specific configuration. We can see the three options, but we will select the first option. Click on **Next**.

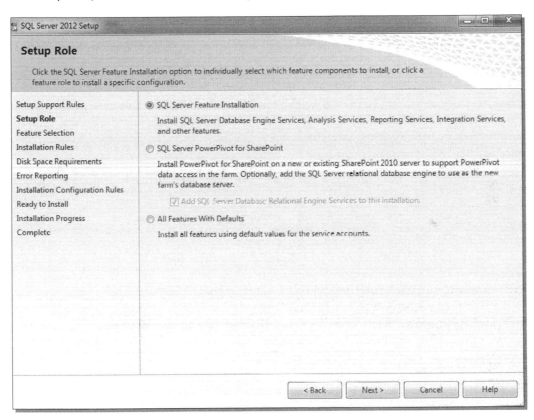

Now you see the **Feature Selection** page where all the services and features are available in SQL Server 2012. Here we select **Database Engine Services** for TestInstance1:

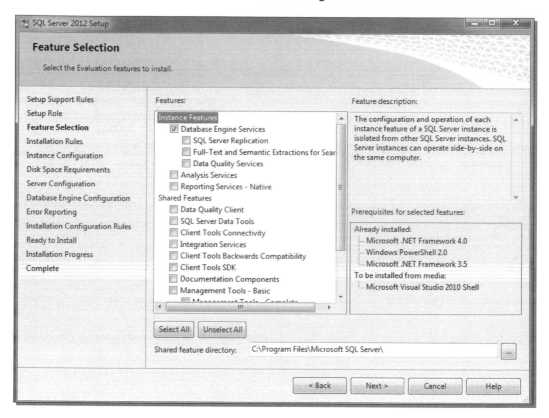

9. On the **Installation Rules** page, we can see the currently running rules. This will determine if the installation will be blocked, and will help us analyze the error; otherwise, click on **Next** to continue.

10. On the **Instance Configuration** screen, put in the instance name and ID for the SQL Server instance and then click on **Next**:

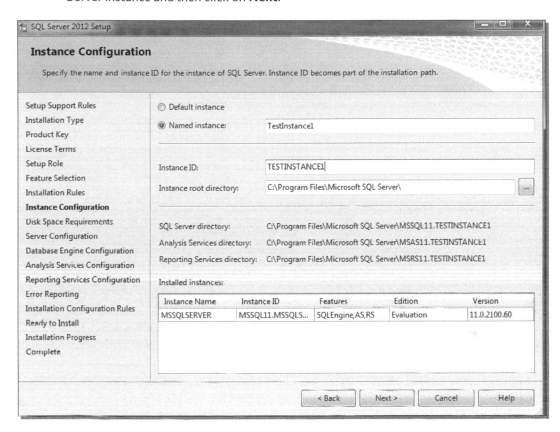

11. In the **Disk Space Requirements** section, we will be able to check the amount of data space needed for the deployment. Click on **Next** to proceed.

12. In the **Server Configuration** wizard, we can review the service accounts and collation configurations.

13. In the **Database Engine Configuration** wizard, we can configure the authentication mode and specify the administrator for the database engine, file stream, and data directories through the **Account Provisioning** option. We can also specify whether the option for `TestInstance1` data directories and file stream should be enabled for the instance or not.

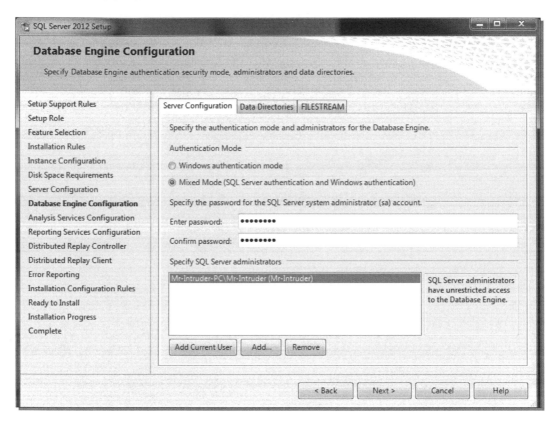

14. In the **Error Reporting** section, we can select the checkbox to automatically send logs to Microsoft in order to improve the future release of SQL Server. Click on **Next** to proceed.

15. In the **Installation Configuration Rules** section, there is a list of rules that are run to determine if the installation process will be blocked. In case there are any issues, we need to first fix them before continuing with the installation. Click on **Next** to proceed.

16. On the **Ready to Install** screen, we can quickly analyze the SQL Server instance configuration and the features that we have selected so far for the deployment. Next, click on the **Install** button to start the installation.

17. We can monitor the progress of the SQL Server instance in the **Installation Progress** wizard. After that is done, click on **Next** to see the summary.

18. On the **Complete** screen, we can review the summary logs and location by clicking on the link that is given below, on the screen. Once the SQL Server database instance is successfully created, just click on the **Close** button to exit from the wizard.

 We must update all the features combined with the SQL Server 2012 instance at the same time, so that when we deploy any services, features, or components for any SQL instance, we are updated.

Next, we are going to discuss the SQL Server database instance level configuration setting. A database administrator decides which type of configuration he/she can implement at the instance level, when we talk about SQL Server. In this section we will discuss the instance level setting (all of these settings can be interchangeable), database engine settings, instance settings, and server settings. The administrator can change the configuration of every instance according to the scenario or requirement through SQL Server Management Studio. These settings will not be applicable on other instances that are hosted on that particular machine. You can just access SQL Server Management Studio, connect to `TestInstance1`, go to the properties of that server, and we will see the configuration settings menu of that instance.

General

This provides general information about the instance, such as the host machine operating system, platform, version, language, memory, processors, root directory, server collation, clustered status, and HARD enable status.

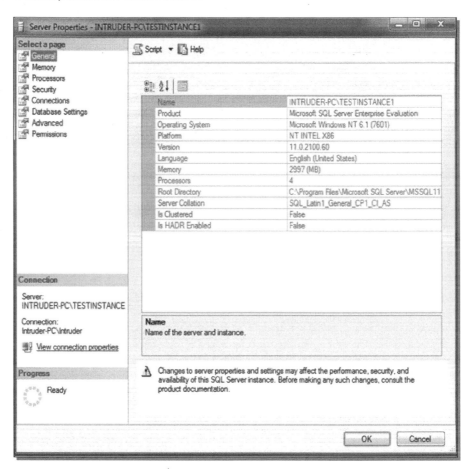

Memory

Here we can configure the memory; for instance, it shows the many options available to configure the server memory in MB with a limit of a minimum and a maximum. Then we see the **Index creation memory** and **Minimum memory per query (in KB)** options. The SQL instance automatically uses the dynamic memory and in this case, the instance requires additional memory. For instance, it will require a host operating system. If we have installed an 86x SQL Server, a minimum memory of 64 MB is used, or if we have a 64-bit server, 128 MB is used. The default memory minimum memory is 0, which means no value is set.

Processors

This section will contain the processor configurations of the instance. Here, we can configure the processor and I/O affinities. The processor affinity assigns the specific server processor to a specific thread, whereas the I/O affinity binds an instance disk I/O to a particular set of CPUs. By default, enable each instance processor configuration for the processor affinity and I/O affinity mask for all processors of the host server. We can configure both the affinities for the same processor.

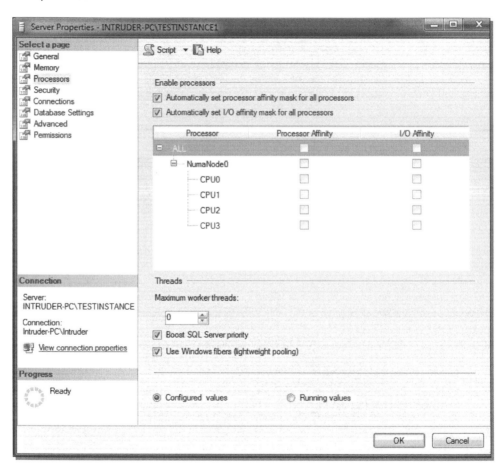

Security

Here we can configure the security settings, such as server authentication, login auditing, server proxy account, common criteria compliance, C audit tracing, and short database ownership chaining, for a specific instance. All these options can be configured as per the requirements of the security policy of a company.

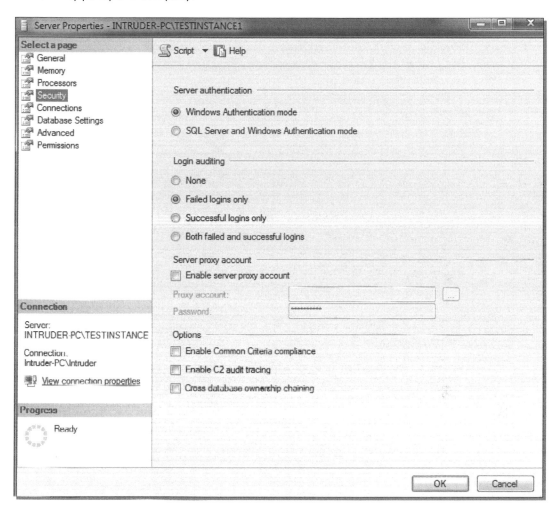

Connections

We can configure many connections through this property. By default, the value is configured to 0, which means unlimited connections, but we can change the number of connections required as per our need. If you want to prevent long-running queries, select the **Use query governor to prevent long-running queries** checkbox. The **Default connection options** section can again be configured as per our needs. The **Remote server connections** section allows another administrator to configure the instance remotely.

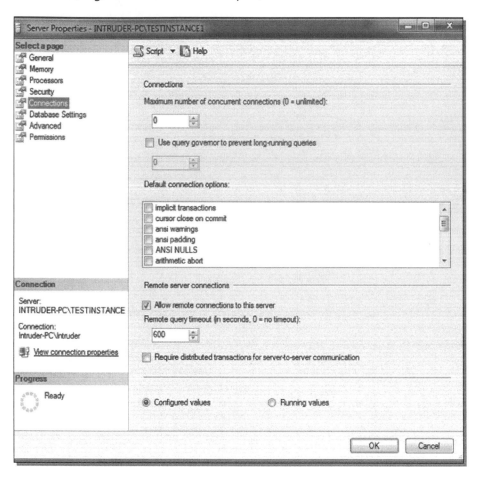

Database Settings

In **Database Settings**, we can configure the default fill factor, media backup retention, the recovery filter, and the database default location. The fill factor decides the percentage of space on each leaf level page that is filled with data. When an index is build or rebuilt, the value we configure is a percentage of fill factors from 1 to 100.

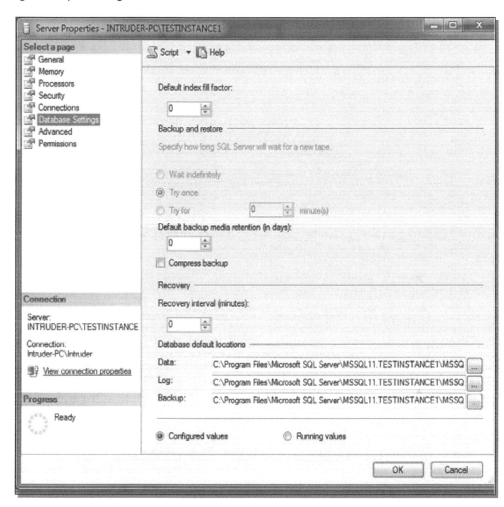

Advanced

In the **Advanced** settings we can configure the file stream options, enable the contained database, trigger firing, set a two-digit cut off, network packet size, and remote logon timeout and parallelism options.

Permissions

In the **Permissions** setting we can configure the permission on the instance level according to users, as every user has different access rights on different instances.

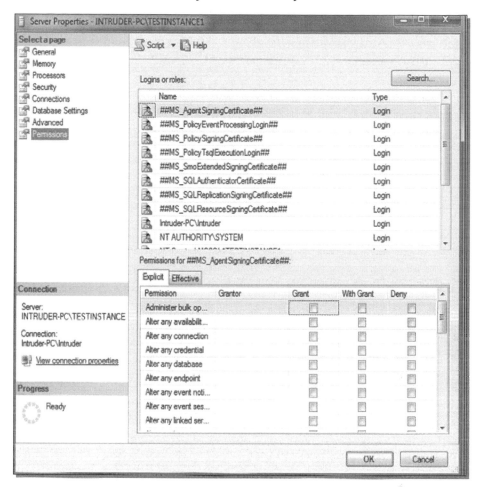

Administrating user management and server roles

In this section we will learn about how the many types of login methods are sustained by SQL and also their authentication types, users, and server roles. All this administration is carried out by **SQL Server Management Studio (SSMS)**.

SQL login

A login provides an authentic connection on a specific instance. We must understand the differences of many SQL Server logins that support the different type of authentication processes. SQL Server 2012 supports four types of authentication processed for users and administrators.

SQL Server Authenticated login

This login is authenticated by the database engine instance instead of the host operating system or domain controller. The login passwords are stored in the master database; we must always configure either the support mixed mode or the SQL Server authentication.

The Windows Authentication login

This type of authentication is supported by the host operating system. In this login, any user can send a login request that the authentication request handles. With this type of authentication, we can map the SQL Server login users who use Windows Authentication with their accounts and groups (local accounts and security groups, domain user accounts, and security groups). We must configure the access to the database administrator, giving him/her the ability to manage memberships of groups.

Certificate authentication

A certificate is a digital security item that contains a public key for SQL Server supported authentication along with an alternative private key. We can generate certificates externally as well as internally through SQL Server. SQL Server's certificates support the IETFX.509V3 certificate standard. Certificate authentications are more powerful because they are used for transporting and importing keys to the X.509 certificate file.

Asymmetric keys

Asymmetric keys are used for securing the symmetric keys, and also for working with private and public keys. It's mainly used for bounded data encryption and digitally signed database objects. This method imports strong name key files that can't be exported as asymmetric keys. It has no expiry options and encryption connection.

Developing dimensions in a SQL Server scenario

A database dimension is a collection of related objects; in other words, attributes. They provide the information about actual data in one or more cubes. Common attributes in product dimensions are product name, product category, line, size, and price. Attributes can be organized into user-assigned hierarchies that provide the paths to assist users when they browse through the data in a cube. By default these attributes are visible as attribute hierarchies, and they can be used to understand fact data in a cube. All these items are bound to more than one column or table in a data source view. A database dimension can be used many times in a cube.

Creating a dimension in a SQL Server development scenario

In this section, we will learn how to create a dimension in a SQL Server development environment. We will apply SQL Server Data Tools to build the dimension by using the **Dimension Wizard** window. We have two ways in which we can build a dimension: with the data source or without it. In this section, we have already built a data source, `ReportServerTestInstance1`, with two tables: `USERS` and `SUBSCRIPTION`. Perform the following steps to create a dimension:

1. Click on SQL Server Data Tools by going to **All programs** in the Start menu and then selecting the SSDT setup. You will see the SSDT wizard on your screen.

2. Go to the **File** menu and click on **New Project**. There we will see the templates (as shown in the following screenshot). Select the Analysis Services with the project name **MultidimensionalProject2**.

3. Click on **OK**.

4. Next, select the `Dimension` folder and right-click and select the **New Dimension**. You will see the **Welcome to the Dimension Wizard** page and then click on **Next**.

5. Now choose the creation method you want to implement in order to create the dimension. We have four methods listed to build a dimension; by default the first option is selected, as shown in the following screenshot:

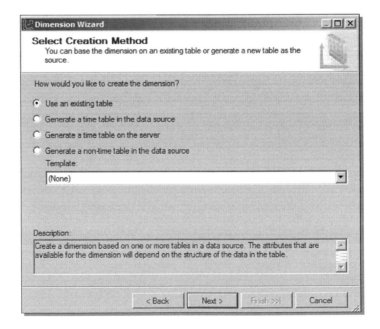

The following is a brief description of the four methods used to create a dimension:

- ○ **Use an existing table**: This builds a dimension based on more than one table in a data connection. The attributes that are available for the dimensions will depend on the structure of the data within the table.

- ○ **Generate a time table in the data source**: This builds a new time dimension table in the underlying data source. The dimension will contain data for the date, range, attribute, and calendar we specify. You must have access to create items in the underlying data source.

- ○ **Generate a time table on the server**: This builds a time dimension table directly on the server, without using an underlying data connection; the dimension will contain data for the date, range, and calendar we specify.

- ○ **Generating a non-time table in the data source**: This builds a native non-time dimension table in the underlying data connection. We must have the permission to create items in the underlying data source; optionally, you can choose to build the dimension using a template.

Here, we have selected the first option.

6. Now we choose the template for the dimension. We will see many templates, so select **Customer Template**, and then click on **Next**:

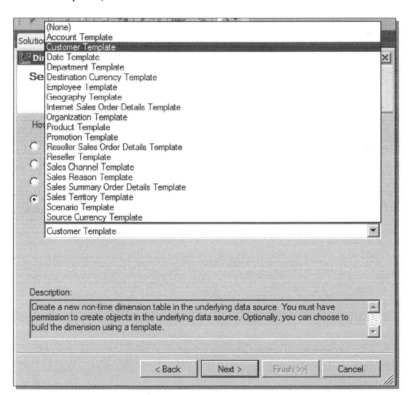

7. Set **Data source view** to `Report ServerTestInstance1`, the **Main table** name to `Users`, and **Key columns** to **UserName** and specify the **Name column** to **UserID**. After this, click on **Next**. This is shown in the following screenshot:

8. Next, specify the dimension attributes and check the **Enable Browsing** checkbox to surface them as hierarchies. Click on **Next**:

9. Now we arrive on the **Completing the Wizard** page, where we enter a name for the native dimension, verify the dimension structure, and then click on **Finish** to save the dimension:

10. After the steps are complete, we see the dimension design as follows:

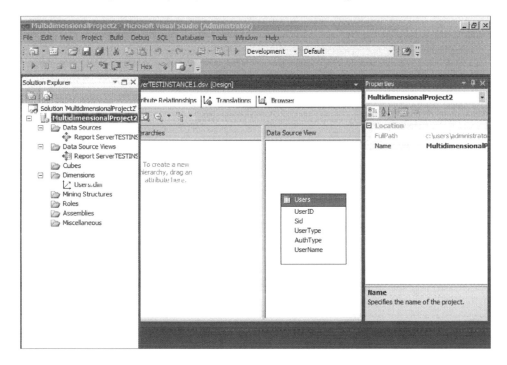

The attribute relationship

A dimension contains a set of attributes that are organized based on the attribute relationships for each table included in that dimension. There is an attribute relationship that relates the table's key attribute to other attributes from that table. We create this relationship when we create the dimension in the database. When we create the attribute relationships, we should also define the unique attribute relationship between the attributes. When any attribute develops an outgoing relation, it must have a unique key relative to its related attribute, for example, Mango: Fruits. In this relationship, the source attribute is Mango and the related attribute is Fruits. An attribute relationship provides some advantages as mentioned in the following list:

✦ This relationship reduces the amount of memory used to speed up the processing of dimensions, partitions, and queries

✦ It increases query performance as storage access is faster and the execution is better optimized

✦ Results of selection are more effective as it is aggregated by the aggregation design algorithm, which provides the user-assigned hierarchies that have been assigned along the relationship path

Developing cubes in a SQL Server scenario

As previously mentioned in the *So, what are SSAS 2012 dimensions and cube?* section, a cube is a multidimensional structure that contains information for analytical purposes; the main constituents of a cube are dimensions and measures. Dimensions define the structure of a cube that you use to slice and dice over, and measures provide the aggregated numerical values of interest to the end user. As a logical structure, a cube allows a client application to retrieve values—of measures—as if they are contained in cells in the cube. The cells are defined for every possible summarized value. A cell, in the cube, is defined by the intersection of dimension members and contains the aggregated values of the measures at that specific intersection.

Creating a cube in a SQL Server development scenario

In this section, we learn how to create a cube in a SQL Server development environment. We apply SQL Server Data Tools to create a cube by using the **Cube Design** wizard. Perform the following steps:

1. Click on SQL Server Data Tools by going to **All programs** in the Start menu and then selecting the SSDT setup. You will see the SSDT wizard on your screen.

2. Select the Cubes folder, right-click on it, and choose **New Cube...**, as shown in the following screenshot:

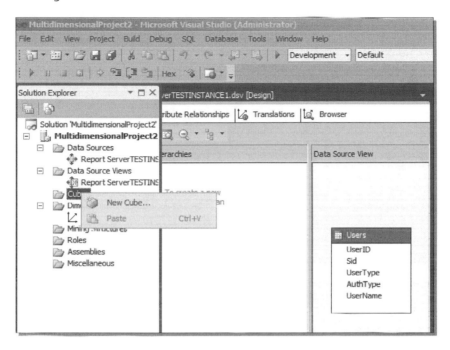

3. Then we will see the **Welcome to the Cube Wizard** page; click on **Next** to continue:

4. Choose the creation method for the cube and also choose the template. Here we have three methods and two templates used to create a cube. We will select the **Use existing tables** option for creating the cube, select the **Adventure Works Enterprise Edition** template, and then click on **Next**:

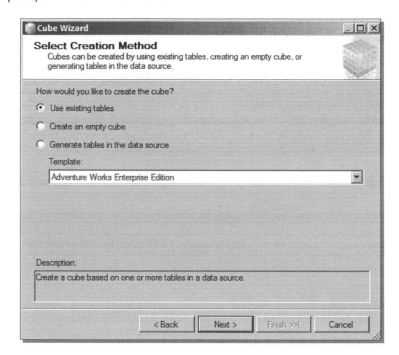

The following is a brief description of the three methods used to create a cube:

- ° **Use an existing table**: This builds a cube based on more than one table in a data connection

- ° **Create an empty cube**: This creates an empty cube, which is useful when users want to create everything manually or when all dimensions are linked dimensions

- ° **Generate tables in the data source**: This builds a table in the underlying data connection (we must have access to build an object in the underlying data source).

5. Here we choose a **Data connection view** value and then choose the tables that will be used as measure groups. Click on **Next** to proceed:

6. Now choose the measures we want to include in the cube, and click on **Next**:

7. Next, select the existing dimension to add to the cube, and then click on **Next**:

8. Select the new dimensions to be created based on the available tables, and then click on **Next**:

9. We will now specify the logical keys for the dimensions based on the table with no keys. Click on **Next**:

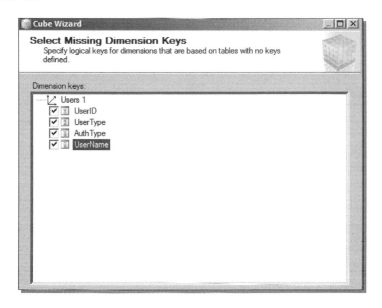

10. Then we arrive on the **Completing the Wizard** page, where we enter the cube name `Report ServerTestInstance1` and preview the structure of the cube. Click on **Finish** to save the cube:

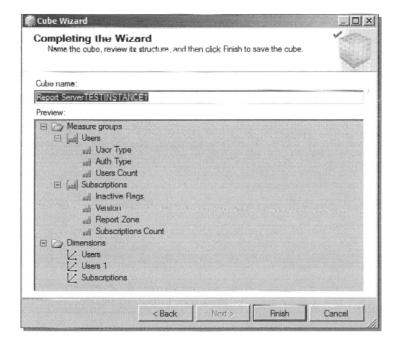

11. Finally, we see the created cube with two fact tables: **Subscriptions** and **Users** with their attributes:

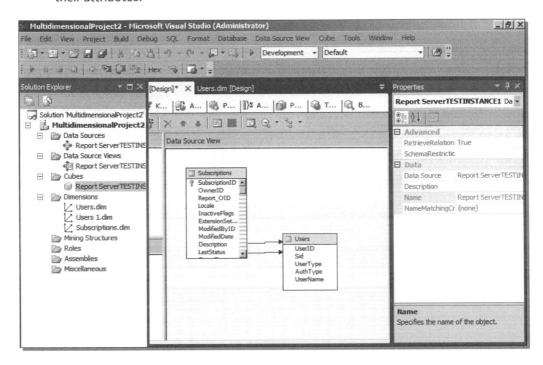

Cube attribute properties

SQL Server provides us the opportunity to specify unique settings for the dimension attributes in cube dimensions based on the same database dimension. The following table describes the properties of a cube attribute:

Property	Description of the property
AggregationUsage	This defines how the Aggregation Design Wizard will design aggregations for the attribute.
AttributeHierarchyEnabled	This verifies if the attribute hierarchy is enabled on this cube dimension. It gives permission to attribute hierarchies to be disabled on specific cubes or dimension roles. This setting has no effect if the active attribute hierarchy is disabled. The default value is **True**.

Property	Description of the property
OptimizedState	This displays the attribute hierarchy that is optimized on the cube dimension. This gives access to attribute hierarchies to be optimized on specific cubes or dimension roles. This setting has no effect if the active attribute hierarchy is not optimized.
AttributeHierarchyVisible	This shows if the attribute hierarchy is visible on this cube dimension. This gives the credentials to attribute hierarchies to be visible on specific cubes or dimension roles. This setting has no effect if the current attribute hierarchy is not visible. The default value is **True**.
AttributeID	This displays the unique ID of the attribute.

In the preceding sections, we learned how to install the additional peripherals of SQL Server 2012. We learned the administration and configuration of a SQL instance, the administration of user management and server roles, and finally the development and creation of the dimensions and cubes in a SQL Server 2012 environment.

Top 5 features you need to know about

In this section we will learn about the top 5 features of SQL Server 2012. These features give a great image to SQL Server and provide benefits to any organization to increase business, such as the Always on availability group feature that provides anytime database access without downtime. Today, data increases daily; a big data support feature provides the option to save unlimited data with Hadoop. A column index store provides a better query search in a SQL environment. For any organization, it is important to show the data to our shareholders, clients, and so on through Power View features as they can present our data in different formats and attractive visualizations, such as charts, bars, and so on.

The top 5 features of SSAS 2012 are as follows:

+ Always on availability group
+ Column store indexes
+ Big data support
+ Contained databases
+ Power view

Always-on availability group

This feature is specially designed for disaster recovery and high availability solutions' alternative to mirroring on an enterprise level. The **Always-on availability group** feature provides maximum availability to a group of user databases on the enterprise. An availability group supports a failover environment for a different group of user databases known as **availability databases**. It supports two types of groups: first is a group of primary databases with read and write access permissions, and second is one to four group secondary databases with read-only access permission or some are backup operations.

In SQL Server, there is an addition to failover clustering enhancement. We will be able to delight a group of databases as a single, more-acquainted-with-today's-common-needs, complex, and multitier database application. The availability group will allow us to failover that group of databases as an entity. Since a specific instance of SQL Server will be able to host multiple groups in the event of failure, we will have the adjustability to failover one accessible group to instance 1, another availability group to instance 2, and so on. That means we don't have a standby server that is capable of managing the full load of our primary server. We can divide those workloads across multiple and lower-powered servers, with the same application transparency we appreciate the traditional mirroring today. It is also adequate to have more than a single replica for every availability group, so we have one or more local backups, which will insure us from localized failures, and one or more remote backups will cover us from whole site failures.

It has support for two alternative accessible modes:

+ **Asynchronous complete mode**: This availability mode is a disaster recovery solutions that works well when the active replicas are distributed over the prefer distances.

+ **Synchronous complete mode**: This active mode provides the high availability and data protection over performance, at the cost of increased transaction latency. A given availability group can support up to three synchronous availability replicas including the current primary replica. It supports the different forms of availability group failover such as default failover, planned manual failover, and forced manual failover along with the default page repair.

Cover against page corruption, encryption, and compression provides a high-performing secure transport. Always-on availability group is not a technology in itself; it is just a great advantage of SQL Server 2012.

Column index store

This is a new feature fully unique to SQL Server 2012 that improves the performance of data warehouse queries on a large scale. A new **Column store index** feature is totally different from regular indexes or heaps; it is specially designed for only read indexes for data warehouse queries. Basically, the database supports two types of data storage: **Row store** and **Column store**. Columns are much easier to search instead of a query searching all data in a row whether data is relevant or not. Column store queries only need to search in columns, which are usually lesser in number, and this increases the search speed.

Think about a covering index that adds multiple columns instead of storing all the various columns in a single row on a single page. Split it up and store every column in its own set of pages. Building a column store index is very easy, and we don't have to learn the syntax of creating them; we just have to mention the **COLUMNSTORE** keyword and put in the data. Always remember once we add the column store in a table we can't delete, update, or insert the data. We just have read-only permission for it. It has a limitation, though, that they have only read access. It means that once a column store index is built in a table, we can no longer implement any DML operations against the table; this makes the advantage far less useful in an OLTP scenario.

The question now is how different is it from a group of indexes on separate columns? It is not that different structurally, except that a column store index is typically assigned on most of the columns in a table. This optimization that has been performed makes a query against multiple columns more capable as compared to a single index, which would be used in conjunction with multiple lookups in a traditional OLTP query.

Big data support

After the PASS conference last year, Microsoft announced the partnership with Apache Hadoop cloud provider. Microsoft released an ODBC driver for SQL Server that will deploy on a Linux platform, and a SQL Server connector for Apache Hadoop. Through these, customers can move large volumes of data between Hadoop and SQL Server 2012. To make use of this thoroughly, we require an advanced data platform that manages data of any type, whether structured or unstructured, and of any size from gigabytes to petabytes.

The big data support solution manages data at rest or in motion. Hadoop gives simplicity, easy management, and an open enterprise-ready Hadoop service that deploy on-premise or in a cloud environment.

Hadoop is a software framework that supports a data-intensive process and enables an application to work with big data support. In technical terms, we can say it comes from MapReduce technologies.

Tidbit

The name **Hadoop** and the yellow elephant come from the yellow toy elephant that co-creator Doug Cutting's son possessed.

Currently, two renowned companies (Yahoo! and Facebook) use Hadoop to process their big data. This platform can solve problems where deep analysis on unstructured and complex data needs to be done at an appropriate time. Microsoft is committed to making Hadoop accessible to a broader class of end users, developers, and IT professionals. Accelerate your Hadoop deployment through the simplicity of Hadoop on Windows.

Contained databases

It is a new characteristic of SQL Server 2012 that is intended to eliminate or reduce the dependencies that a database has on the SQL Server database instance. It enables easy migration of a database to a new database instance with less work involved in validating and reproducing these dependencies. This feature has the capability of assigning a user with a password at the database level. We can change the location of the database to a new server, and applications can change their connecting strings without having to apply new SQL Server login. A common issue that we face today is mismatched security identifiers, but through this feature this issue can be solved. If we use any object in tempdb, we may find that collation conflicts are an important part of our troubleshooting steps, especially when we change the location of the database between SQL Server instances.

In SQL Server, tempdb will automatically create items using the collation of the contained database, instead of the server default. It makes relying on our code easier regardless of the server collation. Contained databases give us an ultimate first step toward database autonomy.

A fully contained database includes metadata and all the settings needed to define the database, and has no configuration dependencies on the database instance of the SQL Server database engine. In the earlier versions of SQL Server, separating databases from the database instance of SQL Server would be time consuming and would require detailed knowledge of the relationship between the database and the SQL instance.

Partially contained databases in SQL Server 2012 make it easier to separate a database from the SQL instance server and other databases. The contained databases consider features with regard to containment. Any user-defined entity that relies only on functions that reside in the database is considered fully contained. Any user-defined entity that relies on functions that reside outside the database is considered uncontained.

Power View

Through this feature we can see the data with interactive data analysis, visualization, and appearance experience. This feature provides modern reporting services for business users, such as data analysts, decision makers, and information workers. This will enable them to easily build and interact with the presentation of data from data models based on PowerPivot workbooks, which already exists in the PowerPivot gallery or tabular model Analysis Services Deploy SQL instance. It is a browser-based Silverlight application introduced by the SharePoint 2010 server that provides the capability to users to present and share with others or their organization through interactive appearances, such as tiles, chart filters, and a number of visualizations, added cards, tiny multiples, and bubble charts.

It always gives a presentable report. We can access our data and present it at any time because we are working on actual data. We don't need to preview our report and check how it looks. It does have a knowledgeable and fullscreen presentation mode, and reporting skills that is fully interactive with clean and highlighting capabilities. We can transport the appearance, for example, modifying our presentation report from Power View to PowerPoint. Each direction of Power View becomes a different PowerPoint slide. Interacting with Power View reports converted to PowerPoint is similar to collaborating with Power Views in Power View reading and fullscreen modes.

In other words, we can say that it is a light web client that drives data in the browser from a data model in the SharePoint server. The model can be a PowerPivot workbook or tabular model active on SQL Server 2012. When we are busy on Power View, we don't require to know the name of the servers or have any type of security access. We don't require to download anything on the machine; it is automatically associated to the data model from which we launched in Power View. The data model acts as a bridge between the complexities of the backend data connection and the preferences of our data.

Concluding this section, I would say that these features have greatly enhanced the SQL Server infrastructure. Every feature has its own benefits, which have increased the business of any organization. SQL Server has other features, but in this section we are just discussing the top 5 features that have really made a huge change in the SQL Server 2012 development environment of any organization.

People and places you should get to know

Here are the must-know official sites, articles, and tutorials, along with communities, where we can gain more knowledge about SQL Server 2012 technologies.

Official sites

✦ Home page: `http://www.microsoft.com/sqlserver/en/us/default.aspx`

✦ Wiki: `http://en.wikipedia.org/wiki/Microsoft_SQL_Server`

✦ Blog: `http://sqlblog.com/tags/SQL+Server+2012/default.aspx`

✦ Source code: `http://www.microsoft.com/betaexperience/pd/SQL2012EvalCTA/enus/default.aspx`

Articles and tutorials

✦ This video tutorial gives information regarding SQL Server 2012 for beginners (`https://www.youtube.com/watch?v=4WEFTQ3VJNg`)

✦ This video tutorial teaches you how to set up SQL Server 2012 (`http://www.youtube.com/watch?v=2aen7PKrGpw&feature=related`)

✦ This tutorial will help you explore the Analysis Services datasheet (`http://www.sql-server-helper.com/sql-server-2012/sql-server-2012-analysis-services-datasheet.aspx`)

✦ This article will help you explore the SQL Server high availablity datasheet (`http://www.sql-server-helper.com/sql-server-2012/sql-server-2012-high-availability.aspx`)

✦ This article will help you explore the SQL Server 2012 Editions and Licensing (`http://www.sql-server-helper.com/sql-server-2012/faq-editions-and-licensing.aspx`)

Community

✦ The official mailing list: `http://sqlcommunity.com/`

✦ Official forums: `http://social.msdn.microsoft.com/Forums/en/category/sqlserver`

✦ Unofficial forums: `http://www.sqlteam.com/forums/`

Thank you for buying
Instant Microsoft SQL Server Analysis Services 2012 Dimensions and Cube

About Packt Publishing

Packt, pronounced 'packed', published its first book "*Mastering phpMyAdmin for Effective MySQL Management*" in April 2004 and subsequently continued to specialize in publishing highly focused books on specific technologies and solutions.

Our books and publications share the experiences of your fellow IT professionals in adapting and customizing today's systems, applications, and frameworks. Our solution based books give you the knowledge and power to customize the software and technologies you're using to get the job done. Packt books are more specific and less general than the IT books you have seen in the past. Our unique business model allows us to bring you more focused information, giving you more of what you need to know, and less of what you don't.

Packt is a modern, yet unique publishing company, which focuses on producing quality, cutting-edge books for communities of developers, administrators, and newbies alike. For more information, please visit our website: www.packtpub.com.

Writing for Packt

We welcome all inquiries from people who are interested in authoring. Book proposals should be sent to author@packtpub.com. If your book idea is still at an early stage and you would like to discuss it first before writing a formal book proposal, contact us; one of our commissioning editors will get in touch with you.

We're not just looking for published authors; if you have strong technical skills but no writing experience, our experienced editors can help you develop a writing career, or simply get some additional reward for your expertise.

SQL Server 2012 with PowerShell V3 Cookbook

ISBN: 978-1-84968-646-4   Paperback: 634 pages

Increase your productivity as a DBA, developer, or IT Pro, by using PowerShell with SQL Server to simplify database management and automate repetitive, mundane tasks

1. Provides over a hundred practical recipes that utilize PowerShell to automate, integrate and simplify SQL Server tasks

2. Offers easy to follow, step-by-step guide to getting the most out of SQL Server and PowerShell

3. Covers numerous guidelines, tips, and explanations on how and when to use PowerShell cmdlets, WMI, SMO, .NET classes or other components

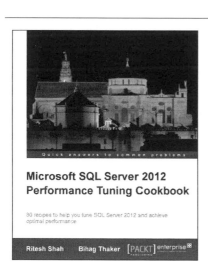

Microsoft SQL Server 2012 Performance Tuning Cookbook

ISBN: 978-1-84968-574-0   Paperback: 478 pages

80 recipes to help you tune SQL Server 2012 and achieve optimal performance

1. Learn about the performance tuning needs for SQL Server 2012 with this book and e-book

2. Diagnose problems when they arise and employ tricks to prevent them

3. Explore various aspects that affect performance by following the clear recipes

Please check **www.PacktPub.com** for information on our titles

![PACKT PUBLISHING]

Microsoft SQL Server 2012 Integration Services: An Expert Cookbook

ISBN: 978-1-84968-524-5   Paperback: 564 pages

Over 80 expert recipes to design, create, and deploy SSIS packages

1. Full of illustrations, diagrams, and tips with clear step-by-step instructions and real time examples

2. Master all transformations in SSIS and their usages with real-world scenarios

3. Learn to make SSIS packages re-startable and robust; and work with transactions

4. Get hold of data cleansing and fuzzy operations in SSIS

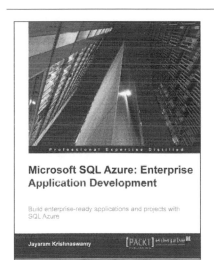

Microsoft SQL Azure: Enterprise Application Development

ISBN: 978-1-84968-080-6   Paperback: 420 pages

Build enterprise-ready applications and projects with SQL Azure

1. Develop large scale enterprise applications using Microsoft SQL Azure

2. Understand how to use the various third party programs such as DB Artisan, RedGate, ToadSoft etc developed for SQL Azure

3. Master the exhaustive Data migration and Data Synchronization aspects of SQL Azure.

Please check **www.PacktPub.com** for information on our titles

Made in the USA
San Bernardino, CA
16 February 2014